21st
Century
Skills Library

REAL WORLD MATH: NATURAL DISASTERS

FLOODS

BY GRAEME DAVIS

CHERRY LAKE
Publishing

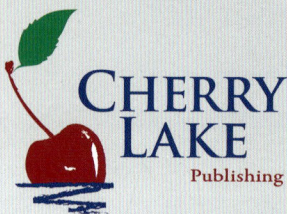

Published in the United States of America by
Cherry Lake Publishing, Ann Arbor, Michigan
www.cherrylakepublishing.com

Content Adviser

Jack Williams
Founding editor of the *USA Today* weather page and author of *The AMS Weather Book: The Ultimate Guide to America's Weather*

Math Adviser

Katherine M. Gregory, M.Ed

Credits

Cover and page 1, ©iStockphoto.com/lhaylett; page 4, ©Fedor Sidorov/
Dreamstime.com; page 6, ©Neil Bradfield/Dreamstime.com; page 8,
©JD/Shutterstock, Inc.; page 10, ©Caitlin Mirra/Shutterstock, Inc.; page 12,
©Nick Saum/Dreamstime.com; page 14, ©Anne Power/Dreamstime.com;
page 17, ©Anne Power/Dreamstime.com; page 19, ©AP Photo/Gerald Herbert;
page 20, ©Jingaiping/Dreamstime.com; page 22, ©AP Photo/ Liang Zhen –
Imaginechina; page 24, ©Del7891/Dreamstime.com; page 27, © Dan70/
Dreamstime.com; page 28, ©iStockphoto.com/Robert Morton

Copyright ©2012 by Cherry Lake Publishing

Library of Congress Cataloging-in-Publication Data
Davis, Graeme, 1958–
  Floods / by Graeme Davis.
     p. cm.—(Real world math)
  Includes bibliographical references and index.
  ISBN 978-1-61080-324-3 (lib.bdg.)—ISBN 978-1-61080-333-5 (e-book)—
ISBN 978-1-61080-409-7 (pbk.)
  1. Floods—Juvenile literature. 2. Flood forecasting—Juvenile literature.
3. Mathematics—Juvenile literature. I. Title. II. Series.
  GB1399.D38 2012
  551.48'9—dc23   2011032620

Cherry Lake Publishing would like to acknowledge
the work of The Partnership for 21st Century Skills.
Please visit *www.21stcenturyskills.org* for more information.

Printed in the United States of America
Corporate Graphics Inc.
January 2012
CLSP10

TABLE OF CONTENTS

CHAPTER ONE
WHAT IS A FLOOD?

Have you ever stood by a river and watched the water gently flowing past you? It's a calming sight, but as you know, not all water moves peacefully. Floods are a huge threat to people and property, and they are more common than you

River water is constantly moving.

might think. In fact, floods make up 40 percent of all natural disasters. But how do floods occur, and what can we do to limit their destruction?

Water is moving around our planet all the time. Sunlight heats lakes and seas, causing their waters to **evaporate**. **Water vapor**, the gas produced when water evaporates, rises and forms clouds. Wind moves the clouds until they are cool enough to drop their water as rain, snow, sleet, or hail. The rain or melted snow runs into streams and rivers, and goes back into the sea or lakes. This process, called the **water cycle**, then starts all over again.

21ST CENTURY CONTENT

The Advanced Hydrologic Prediction Service is run by scientists at the National Oceanic and Atmospheric Administration (NOAA). It collects data from thousands of measuring devices owned by hundreds of federal, state, and local agencies. The devices include rain and river gauges, automated weather stations, and satellites. NOAA supercomputers use this data to produce flood prediction models for more than 2,500 locations throughout the United States.

Floods occur when water comes into an area more quickly than the local streams and rivers can move it out. Heavy rainfall is one cause of flooding, but there are others. **Storm surges**, **tsunamis**, **debris**, a dam failure, and even climate change can cause floods.

A storm surge is seawater that is pushed ashore by high winds during a hurricane or tropical storm. In low-lying areas near the coast, it can be a real danger.

Storms sometimes cause huge waves to form.

REAL WORLD MATH CHALLENGE

According to the UNESCO International Flood Initiative, about 520 million people live in areas where there is a risk of flooding. Recent figures from the U.S. Census Bureau show that the world's total population is close to 7 billion people. How many people live in areas that are not at risk of floods?

The following table gives the cost of flood damage in the United States from 2001 to 2010. What is the total dollar loss in the last 10 years?

Year	Cost
2010	$5.04 billion
2009	$1.03 billion
2008	$7.40 billion
2007	$2.88 billion
2006	$4.25 billion
2005	$49.66 billion
2004	$17.28 billion
2003	$3.26 billion
2002	$1.63 billion
2001	$10.14 billion

(Turn to page 29 for the answers)

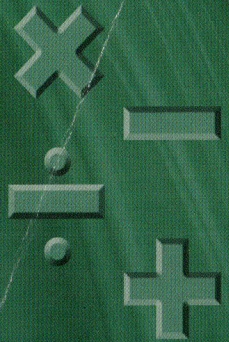

A tsunami is a huge wave caused by an underwater earthquake or volcano. Tsunamis can travel at more than 500 miles (805 kilometers) per hour and reach over 100 feet (30 meters) in height when they hit shore.

Debris can be any material, such as **silt** or garbage, that blocks a stream or river and prevents water from moving out. Rivers swollen by heavy rainfall often carry debris with them. When the debris chokes the river, the flooding becomes worse.

Large amounts of debris can cause floods.

Dam failure rarely happens, but when it does, it can cause tremendous damage and loss of life. Dams hold back huge bodies of water. When the structure fails, the water that has built up behind the dam rushes out, causing floods until it drains away.

Climate change may cause floods in two different ways. As the earth becomes warmer, ice melts at the North and South Poles, adding more water into the oceans. As ocean levels rise, low-lying coastal areas are slowly being covered by water. Secondly, since global warming makes the atmosphere more humid, more rain and snow is formed and dropped on the planet.

Smaller floods occur frequently. For example, workers may accidentally break a water pipe. Sometimes, the dams built by beavers can stop up small streams and flood the surrounding area.

CHAPTER TWO
WHERE DO FLOODS HAPPEN?

Floods can happen wherever water flows. Low-lying river valleys and coastal areas are most at risk, but floods can even

Hurricane Katrina caused serious flooding in New Orleans, Louisiana.

happen in mountains and deserts. All it takes is too much water. The areas that suffer most from flooding are river **deltas** and **flood plains**.

LIFE & CAREER SKILLS

The U.S. Federal Emergency Management Agency (FEMA) was established to prepare for and respond to disasters of all types. These include natural disasters such as floods, hurricanes, earthquakes, and tornadoes. You can check out FEMA's advice on what to do if a flood strikes your area by visiting *www.fema.gov/hazard/flood/index.shtm*. The National Weather Service offers flood forecasts for the entire nation at *http://water.weather.gov/ahps/rfc/rfc.php*. Just click on the area where you live to find out the latest river conditions, rainfall and snowfall levels, and the flood outlook in your area.

New Orleans, Louisiana, is built on the Mississippi River delta. In 2005, the city suffered very bad floods as a result of Hurricane Katrina. The Ganges Delta covers parts of India and Bangladesh and also suffers from regular floods. Some delta floods are caused by a storm surge, and others by heavy rainfall making the river waters rise.

A flood plain holds the extra water when a river rises over its banks. Most rivers have flood plains, except where they flow through canyons. The flood plain of a major river such as the Mississippi can be up to 80 miles (129 km) wide.

The Mississippi floods every year.

Floods would be less dangerous if people didn't live on flood plains or deltas. The land in those areas, however, is very valuable, and large numbers of people often live and farm there. These lands are usually very good for growing crops because over millions of years, rivers have deposited rich **alluvial** soil on them. Deltas attract people and businesses because they are good places to build ports. New Orleans is built on a river delta. So are Rotterdam in the Netherlands and Shanghai in China. Each year, trillions of dollars' worth of trade flows through these important ports.

REAL WORLD MATH CHALLENGE

Areas with higher flood risks often produce larger amounts of crops. Louisiana is on a river delta with a high flood risk. Montana is a mountainous state with a lower flood risk. Both states produce crops such as wheat, corn, and hay. Look at the chart below. What is the difference between Louisiana's production and Montana's production for each crop?

| Crop | 2010 Yield Per Acre | |
	Louisiana	Montana
Wheat	50.0 bushels	41.3 bushels
Corn	140.0 bushels	135.0 bushels
Hay	2.8 tons	2.1 tons

(Turn to page 29 for the answers)

CHAPTER THREE
DO THE MATH: MISSISSIPPI FLOODS

The Mississippi river system is the largest in North America. It collects most of the water that falls between the Rocky

Towns along the Mississippi River must always be prepared for a flood.

Mountains and the Appalachians. It carries this water south to the Gulf of Mexico. Every second, nearly 3.3 million gallons (12.5 million liters) of water flow out of the Mississippi and into the Gulf.

The water level of the Mississippi is always high in spring. That's when melting snow from the upper Midwest adds to the river's normal load of water. In April and May 2011, four major storm systems hit the Midwest and the South. The storms dropped even more water, which eventually found its way into the Mississippi River.

The rising waters hit Missouri and Illinois first. The U.S. Army Corps of Engineers blew a hole 2 miles (3.2 km) wide in a **levee** just south of Cairo, Illinois. This allowed the water to flood nearby farmland. If they had not done this, the town would have been flooded.

In Tennessee, some suburbs of Memphis were flooded, but the town itself was spared. Interstate 40 was underwater between Memphis and Little Rock, Arkansas. Further downstream, in Vicksburg, Mississippi, the river rose to its highest level in 183 years. Fields and some of the lower-lying parts of town were flooded. The flow of the river was estimated to be 17 million gallons (64.3 million L) per second, more than five times its normal flow.

New Orleans was saved by its flood defenses. By opening the Morganza **Spillway**, almost 1.2 million gallons (4.5 million L) of water per second was **diverted** away from the city. Nearby land was flooded and some communities were evacuated, but the flooding was not as bad as some people had feared. The Bonnet Carré Spillway was also opened, sending water into Lake Pontchartrain.

The worst impact of the flood was the damage it did to farmland. Many of the farmers lost their crops for the entire year. Without crops to sell, these farmers had little or no income. The destroyed crops caused a shortage of some foods, resulting in price increases across the nation.

LEARNING & INNOVATION SKILLS

Imagine that you are in charge of a spillway, and there is a big flood coming. Will you open the spillway or not? If you open it, thousands of acres of farmland will be destroyed. Many local farmers will lose money. Some may lose their homes, their property, and everything else they own. If you leave it closed, the flood might overtake the town and cause even more damage. What will you do? Why?

Spillways help control where floodwaters go.

Farmers, however, were not the only ones to suffer. The floods stopped local businesses from operating, costing them millions of dollars. Some businesses could not take the losses, and they closed for good. Many workers lost their jobs. Thousands of buildings were damaged or destroyed. The total cost of the damage was about $4 billion.

REAL WORLD MATH CHALLENGE

Opening the Morganza Spillway diverted 1.2 million (1,200,000) gallons of water per second away from New Orleans. If the flood was bringing 17 million (17,000,000) gallons per second toward the city, how much water was still headed for New Orleans? How many times more was this than the normal rate of 3.3 million (3,300,000) gallons per second?

(Turn to page 29 for the answers)

ROSPERITY ST

PRINCEVILLE RD

Many towns near the Morganza Spillway experienced severe flooding.

CHAPTER FOUR
DO THE MATH: CHINA UNDER WATER

The Yangtze River drains water from roughly one-fifth of China. It is about 250 miles (402 km) longer than the Mississippi River. About one-third of China's population lives

Many of China's largest cities are located along the Yangtze River.

near the river. In June 2011, heavy rains caused the Yangtze and other rivers in central and southern China to rise. As the weeks passed, dozens of cities were flooded, and hundreds of thousands of people were evacuated. On June 8, 4.8 inches (122 millimeters) of rain fell in a single hour on Wangmo County in Guizhou Province, breaking a 200-year-old record. Hunan Province had its worst rains in 300 years.

REAL WORLD MATH CHALLENGE

Hectares are a unit of area in the metric system. One hectare is equal to 2.47 acres or 0.003861 square miles. The floods destroyed 1.16 million hectares of crops in China in June 2011. How many acres is that? How many square miles?

China's currency is the yuan. One yuan is worth $0.155, or 15.5 cents. What is the dollar equivalent of 43.2 billion yuan of damage?

(Turn to page 29 for the answers)

To make matters worse, two tropical storms hit the coast of central China. They brought more rain and high winds, which drove seawater ashore, adding to the floods. Further inland, the rain caused landslides. The ground became **saturated** and flowed downhill in rivers of mud and rocks. Roads were blocked or washed away, making things harder for rescue workers.

By the end of June, China's State Flood Control and Drought Relief Headquarters reported that at least 239 people had died in the floods and 86 people were missing. In total, more than 36 million people were affected by the disaster. The floods destroyed about 107,000 houses and almost 1.16 million hectares of crops. In June alone, the floods cost China's economy 43.2 billion yuan.

People used boats to travel through city streets during the 2011 floods in China.

21ST CENTURY CONTENT

Water is not the only problem caused by floods. The Centers for Disease Control and Prevention lists these additional hazards:

- Storms and floods can bring down power lines. Water conducts electricity, so if a power line touches water, it can be very dangerous.
- People wading through a flood cannot see what is under their feet. They may injure themselves on broken glass or other objects under the water.
- Floods and heavy rains can cause landslides, which can bury buildings and destroy roads.
- Sewage, rotting crops, and other things can contaminate floodwaters. This can lead to outbreaks of disease and infection.
- Food can become scarce when floods wash out fields of crops, leading to malnutrition and even starvation.
- People are not the only ones affected by a flood. Wild animals can be dangerous, especially when they are running from a disaster. Even pets and farm animals can panic and be more likely to attack humans.

CHAPTER FIVE
DEFENSE AGAINST FLOODS

Because floods can be so dangerous, it is not surprising that people have built flood defenses to protect themselves and their homes. Let's take a look at some types of flood defenses in four different countries.

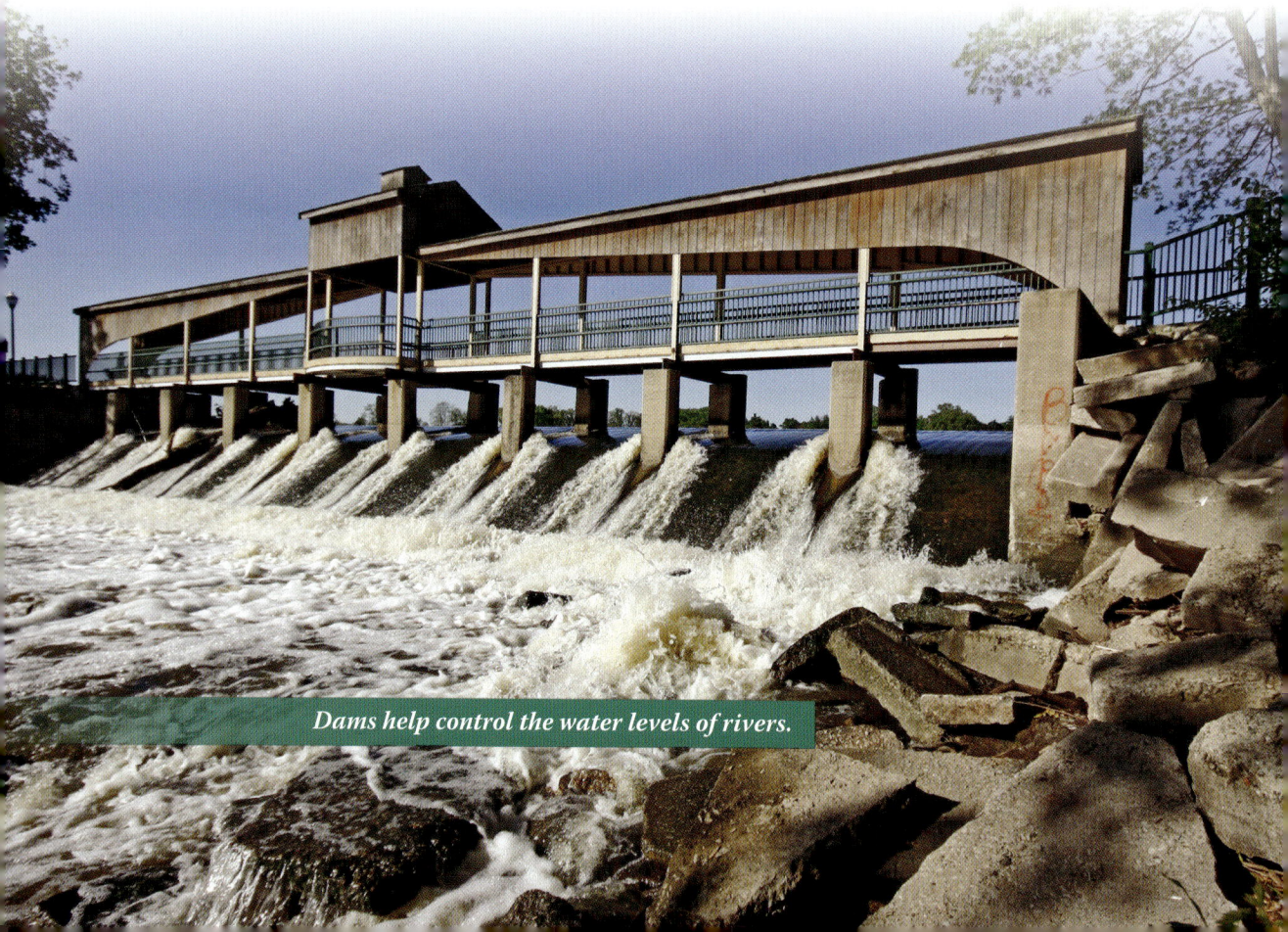

Dams help control the water levels of rivers.

The Mississippi's flood defenses focus on water coming down the river. Levees keep the river from overflowing. Spillways divert water into areas where flooding will do less damage. The Mississippi River has more than 2,000 miles (3,218 km) of levees. There are another 2,500 miles (4,023 km) of levees on the river's main **tributaries**. The Morganza Spillway is 3,900 feet (1,188 meters) long and has 125 gates. In May 2011, it diverted up to 114,000 cubic feet (3,228 cubic meters) of water per second out of the river.

LEARNING & INNOVATION SKILLS

Some people believe that China's Three Gorges Dam causes as many problems as it solves. The water trapped by the dam has filled up the valley behind it, forcing 1.4 million people to move out. A number of important archaeological sites in the valley are now underwater. Some scientists say that pollution is building up in the water behind the dam. If a dam were built near your home, what problems might it solve? What problems might it cause?

In England, London's Thames Barrier was built to deal with the high tides and storm surges that can bring water up the Thames River to flood the city of London. The Thames Barrier has four main gates. Each gate can be raised to block water from coming upstream.

REAL WORLD MATH CHALLENGE

Each gate in the Thames Barrier is 61 meters wide. If 1 meter is 39.4 inches, how wide is each gate in feet? Each gate is 66 feet high. What is a gate's height in meters? Don't forget to convert between inches and feet!

Measurement	Meters	Feet
Length	61	?
Height	?	66

(Turn to page 29 for the answers)

The Netherlands occupies the delta of the Rhine River, one of Europe's largest rivers. Much of the Netherlands is actually below sea level. Its famous dikes and windmills are old-fashioned flood defenses. The Delta Works is a huge system of dikes, levees, and barriers that protect the delta area. The Oosterschelde storm surge barrier, one part of the Delta Works, is more than 9,193 feet (2,800 m) long.

The Rhine is about 765 miles
(1,231 km) long.

In China, the Three Gorges Dam was built to control floods on the Yangtze River. It uses water turbines to generate electricity, making it the world's biggest power plant as well as a flood defense. The dam is 1.4 miles (2.3 km) wide and 575 feet (175 m) high.

Floods have occurred throughout Earth's history. As technology has improved, so have our flood defenses. Who knows what methods and materials will be used to protect the land from flood damage in the future?

The Three Gorges Dam was completed in 2006.

REAL WORLD MATH CHALLENGE ANSWERS

Chapter One

Page 7

6.48 billion people live in areas that are not at risk of floods.

$7,000,000,000 - 520,000,000 = 6,480,000,000$, or 6.48 billion

$102.57 billion was lost in 10 years.

$5.04 + 1.03 + 7.40 + 2.88 + 4.25 + 49.66 + 17.28 + 3.26 + 1.63 + 10.14 = \$102.57$ billion

Chapter Two

Page 13

Louisiana produces 8.7 more bushels of wheat than Montana.

$50.0 - 41.3 = 8.7$ bushels

Louisiana produces 5 more bushels of corn.

$140.0 - 135.0 = 5$ bushels

Louisiana produces 0.7 more tons of hay.

$2.8 - 2.1 = 0.7$ tons

Chapter Three

Page 18

15,800,000 gallons per second were still going toward New Orleans.

$17,000,000 - 1,200,000 = 15,800,000$ gallons

This amount is 4.8 times more than usual.

$15,800,000 \div 3,300,000 = 4.8$

Chapter Four

Page 21

1.16 million hectares is 2,865,200 acres.

$1,160,000 \times 2.47 = 2,865,200$

1.16 million hectares is 4,479 square miles.

$1,160,000 \times 0.003861 = 4,478.8$

43.2 billion yuan is equal to $6.696 billion

$43,200,000,000 \times 0.155 = 6,696,000,000$

Chapter Five

Page 26

Each gate in the Thames Barrier is 200 feet wide.

61 meters $\times 39.4 = 2,403.4$ inches

$2,403.4$ inches $\div 12 = 200.283$ feet

Each gate is 20 meters high.

66 feet $\times 12 = 792$ inches

792 inches $\div 39.4 = 20.1$ meters

GLOSSARY

alluvial (uh-LOO-vee-uhl) a type of soil deposited by rivers

debris (duh-BREE) a mixture of broken materials

deltas (DEL-tuhz) flat, muddy areas where rivers flow into the sea

diverted (di-VUR-tid) changed the direction of a moving object

evaporate (i-VAP-uh-rate) when a liquid changes into a vapor or gas

flood plains (FLUHD PLAYNZ) flat areas beside a river

levee (LEV-ee) a built-up riverbank

saturated (SAH-chuh-ray-ted) soaked thoroughly or filled completely

silt (SILT) very fine rock particles carried by a river

spillway (SPIL-way) a gate that diverts water away from a river

storm surges (STORM SUR-jiz) seawater pushed onto land by a storm

tributaries (TRIH-byuh-ter-eez) rivers that flow into a larger river

tsunamis (tsoo-NAH-meez) large, fast-moving waves caused by underwater earthquakes or volcanoes

water cycle (WAH-tur SYE-kuhl) the constant movement of the earth's waters

water vapor (WAH-tur VAY-pur) the gas produced when water evaporates

FOR MORE INFORMATION

BOOKS

Kent, Deborah. *The Great Mississippi Flood of 1927*. New York: Children's Press, 2009.

Kusky, Timothy. *The Hazardous Earth: Floods*. New York: Facts on File, 2008.

Raum, Elizabeth. *Surviving Floods*. Chicago: Heinemann-Raintree, 2012.

WEB SITES

Advanced Hydrologic Prediction Service
www.weather.gov/os/water/ahps/hydro/AMS_background_2.pdf
An online brochure about the scientists who try to predict floods.

Environment Agency—The Thames Barrier
www.environment-agency.gov.uk/homeandleisure/floods/38353.aspx
For information on London's high-tech flood defenses.

How Stuff Works: Three Gorges Dam
http://science.howstuffworks.com/environmental/green-science/three-gorges-dam-disaster.htm
An in-depth review of the pros and cons of China's Three Gorges Dam.

INDEX

ABOUT THE AUTHOR

Graeme Davis grew up in England beside the Thames River, but is happy that he was never affected by a flood. Today he is married and lives in Virginia. He has written over 70 books and also works in the video games industry, where he puts his math skills to use every day.